T0151170

"WHAT I HAVE WRITTEN"
—PONTIUS PILATE

"WHAT I HAVE WRITTEN"
—PONTIUS PILATE

BILL GLASS

Advantage

Published by Advantage, Charleston, South Carolina.
Member of Advantage Media Group.

ADVANTAGE is a registered trademark, and the Advantage colophon is a trademark of Advantage Media Group, Inc.

Printed in the United States of America.

10 9 8 7 6 5 4 3 2 1

ISBN: 978-1-64225-215-6
LCCN: 2020915142

Cover artwork by Amy Canada.
Cover design by Carly Blake.
Layout design by Megan Elger.

This publication is designed to provide accurate and authoritative information in regard to the subject matter covered. It is sold with the understanding that the publisher is not engaged in rendering legal, accounting, or other professional services. If legal advice or other expert assistance is required, the services of a competent professional person should be sought.

Advantage Media Group is proud to be a part of the Tree Neutral® program. Tree Neutral offsets the number of trees consumed in the production and printing of this book by taking proactive steps such as planting trees in direct proportion to the number of trees used to print books. To learn more about Tree Neutral, please visit **www.treeneutral.com**.

TreeNeutral

Advantage Media Group is a publisher of business, self-improvement, and professional development books and online learning. We help entrepreneurs, business leaders, and professionals share their Stories, Passion, and Knowledge to help others Learn & Grow. Do you have a manuscript or book idea that you would like us to consider for publishing? Please visit **advantagefamily.com** or call **1.866.775.1696**.

I dedicate this book to Mavis,
Mindy, Billy, and Bobby.

CONTENTS

ACKNOWLEDGEMENTS

Mrs. Jane Preston, Miki Canada, Amy Canada, and Tony Woodlin

INTRODUCTION

"What I have written, I have written" (John 19:19–22 NIV). Pontius Pilate was the fifth governor of the Roman province of Judaea, serving under Emperor Tiberius from 26 to 36 CE. He was speaking of the inscription he had ordered to be nailed to the cross that read, "THIS IS JESUS, THE KING OF THE JEWS!" (Matthew 27:37 NASB).

The Sadducees and Pharisees demanded that the accusation should be changed to read that He *claimed* to be the King of the Jews. But Pontius Pilate said, "What I have written, I have written," and he would not change it

(John 19:21–22 NIV). The cross laid it out for the world to see. He was the Beginning and the End, the Son of God who laid down His life for the world! Does this mean that Pilate was saved? I think that the answer could be *yes*, because he clearly stated that Jesus was the Son of God. Whether he took Jesus at His word and applied it to his life is debatable. But God said if you have faith as small as a mustard seed, then nothing will be impossible for you (Matthew 17:20).

"What I have written, I have written." That statement could be said by all of us, because what we have written in the lives of others is irrefutable. Our lives are an open book that preaches the truth or a lie. We write the truth, or a lie, to all that we have within our sphere of influence, especially our families. In the case of Pontius Pilate, he has continued to testify to the truth for over two thousand years, even though he at first may have spoken in a mocking way. Just as he stood by the words on the sign nailed to the cross, I pray that what I have written in my own life will point others to our Lord.

Pilate was a ruler over Judaea during the time of Christ. There was a centurion by the cross who said, "This man truly was the Son of God!" (Matthew 27:54 NLT). Were Pilate and the centurion truly converted? I don't know, but they seemed to be convicted enough to believe that Jesus Christ was for real. Whether or not they called him their Savior is debatable, but I am convinced that they were certainly touched by him. So Pilate's faith was not shaken by the Pharisaic protest that Christ claimed to be the Son of God. If it was a half-hearted confession, he wouldn't have stood by it so strongly. Strangely, we don't hear of him or the centurion ever being mentioned again in the Bible. It seems to me that someone as great as Pilate would have appeared again, so

CHAPTER 1
NO DECAPITATIONS!

In the movie *The Case for Christ*, the question is asked: why did Jesus allow Himself to be crucified? After all, He was God, and He could have stopped the crucifixion. But He didn't. Why? That's easy—love! It was love that showed how much He loved us, the love of the great Creator who by His own hand had created us. In essence, He has said, "I made you in My own image, and I loved you so much I chose to die for you because of your sin." He had to become sin for us, but in order to do this, He had to lower Himself and become like us. He had to put on a bodysuit and became a man known as Jesus. He limited Himself and became like us so that it was possible for Him to suffer like we suffer.

More than that, His scars were painful. God was fragile when He was in Jesus's form. It was tough, and He hurt just like we hurt. The God-man did this. It is difficult to believe—but by faith we do believe! God became man, the man Jesus. As a human, He could feel the pain of the cross. Crucifixion was the worst possible death. The pain from the nails was unimaginably intense. The wood of the cross had splinters that ripped His back almost as much as the beating. He took the beating with a stone-embedded whip, which tore into his back and side, causing blood to ooze from every pore. From the crown of thorns, He was blinded by His own blood flowing down from His forehead. The pain of being nailed to the cross was excruciating.

A little boy built a toy boat, which he put in a ditch that led to a stream that continued out into the ocean. When the boy found the boat gone, he followed the stream to the ocean and realized what had happened. He later found his boat in a pawnshop and had to pay a high price to buy the boat back. But he said to himself, "Little boat, I made you, I lost you, I found you, and now I bought you back. So you are twice mine!"

That is exactly what God was saying: "I made you in creation, I lost you in sin, and I bought you back by crucifixion."

Jesus was hurt even more by the rejection of the very people that He was dying for—He came to His own and was rejected by them (John 1:11). Christ says exactly the same thing as the little boy: "I made you in creation, I lost you—you went your own way in sin—and I bought you back on the cross. Now you are *twice* mine." It wasn't enough for Him to just say it. He had to show us by dying.

> It wasn't enough for Him to just say it. He had to show us by dying.

In marriage, it's not enough to just say, "I love you." You must prove it to your wife by providing a loving home for her and your children. It is not only meeting their needs but also gifting them with nice things like jewelry, nice clothes, vacations, and taking the time to have fun together. This is the prerequisite for all types of love. We have to show it!

A positive word is always the right thing to say to acknowledge a hurt. A faith-filled response is even better. At funerals, the pastor speaks of Heaven. In the hospital, he affirms God's power to heal. In settling conflicts, he speaks of forgiving each other. Then he encourages hugging, kissing, and forgetting harsh words or past differences.

Instead of a lie, speak the truth. In death, speak resurrection! In satanic attacks, speak God's word. In weakness, speak of God's power and your personal power through the Holy Spirit.

Scripture tells us, "I can do all things through Him" and "I have become all things to all people so that by all possible means I might save some" (Phil. 4:13 ESV; 1 Corinthians 9:22 NIV). Don't glorify Satan, glorify God.

Nik Wallenda walked across that great canyon in Nicaragua, but he gave the *glory to God* as he walked the wire while wearing a gas mask. The wire shook from the wind as poisonous smoke erupted out of the huge volcano. But despite it all, he gave glory to God!

Billy Graham preached to millions on TV. Nik Wallenda also preached to millions on worldwide television while walking a tiny wire. What a witness!

But I invite you to picture a little mother slaving away in her kitchen that same morning in a poverty-stricken slum in that same Nicaraguan area. There she was, trying to be a godly wife to her husband and loving mother to her children! What she was doing was not as spectacular as Wallenda on the tightrope, not as amazing, but just as pleasing to God. She didn't have the audience of millions that he had, but she still fulfilled the "go ye therefore" Christian command.

Will there be others who attempt great feats for God's glory? Absolutely. I was praying for Nik that day as he made his record walk into the history books for height and distance, and he was amazing!

Over fifty years ago, I was doing much the same kind of thing, because I was one of the early Christian football players who was attempting to use the popularity of pro football to be a witness for Christ. I sought to use that platform to conduct citywide stadium crusades. It was Billy Graham himself who challenged me to capitalize on the great witness opportunity that football provided. God blessed me with four trips to the Pro Bowl and a world championship, which brought me an invitation to speak at several Billy Graham crusades. This allowed multiple opportunities to make my witness felt nationally and internationally.

God had plans, not just for conducting citywide crusades, but for sending us into prisons as well. I say, "Go git 'em, Wallenda. The world awaits your witness. But I must caution you—when I 'fell' in football, it only cost me an occasional fifteen-yard penalty. But if *you* fall, it could cost you your *life!*" Evidently his grandfather waited too long to retire from walking the tightrope, and it did cost him his life when he fell from a poorly rigged tightrope football. Thankfully neither I nor my family have had to sue them for brain damage or for my premature death. But along the way, I have been thrilled to hear of many people who have been influenced by my witness as well as that of other Christian athletes, and *that's* the goal.

If Christians were to take the Wallenda challenge and set the goal of giving their best in their field of endeavor, then all Christian leaders would rise to the task and be the best they could possibly be in all their affairs. Their witness would spill over into every area of life.

A woman must find a Christian man to marry who will work hard and won't cheat on her. I'm reminded of one woman who had enough when her husband cheated on her. She thought if he did it once he would probably do it again. Their marriage ended in divorce. She decided to look for a Christian man who would never cheat on her—one who had a total commitment to God and to their marriage and who would be a hardworking provider as well.

Christian employees would never steal from their boss or the company. They wouldn't rationalize theft or stolen hours from the workplace that they didn't earn. Having a true commitment to Christ should cause any employee to imitate Christ always by being dependable, reliable, and trustworthy. Why? Because of the devotion they have to Christ, allowing His love to change them from the inside out. Another way to look at it is that they work for God. Would you steal or lie to God? Obviously, no!

People of God should be Christians to the core, because to fail at being a good employee is to be a bad witness.

People of God should be Christians to the core, because to fail at being a good employee is to be a bad witness. Even in the NFL, if I failed to play hard, I was being a poor Christian. If the play called for a sack on the quarterback, I sacked him, causing him to miss the pass or fumble the ball (for Christ's sake). Often the TV commentator would say something like, "That was the gentle giant Bill Glass, a seminary student in the off-season, who just slammed the quarterback to the ground and caused the fumble!" This was all legal, but no letup of my responsibility! I often quoted the familiar scripture (while humorously yelling), "The meek shall inherit the earth" (Matthew 5:5 NIV), referring to the quarterback, who would be paid a much higher salary than any defensive lineman. I wasn't above using salary differences as a motivation to dislike the opposition players, but never to the point of playing dirty. I even made friends with other teams' players off the field, but certainly *not* during the game. In the heat of the battle, I always tried to maintain a dislike

CHAPTER 2
HEAVENLY JET-PROPELLED MIND

Death—I'm looking forward to Heaven and being with Christ; my wife, Mavis; and all those who beat me there. What a reunion—no more pain in my dying process! No earthly limitations, only the joy of Heaven's freedom. I can't wait! I know it will be fun to let those I love show me around. Football and ministry teammates will be gathered there, along with inmates who are now free—no walls, no bars, no crime, no desire to escape. True freedom for all believers with joy unspeakable and full of glory! No fake joy—only real, limitless joy, and answers even to those questions that I didn't know needed to be answered!

Earthly and selfish urges will be replaced 100 percent with His overwhelming presence of love. There will be such satisfaction and fulfillment of joy and peace, but it gets better. Infinitely better! God's love is always over-the-top better! No tears or sorrow or pain or sickness or loneliness—just joy, peace, and fulfillment. Task attempted and achieved, limitless knowledge and understanding of all things that were a puzzle to me on earth! But now I *see* and believe, not with my slowed-down earthly brain, but with my heavenly jet-propelled mind! New and different questions flood my thinking, and answers come that only God knew before, but now, in Heaven, *I* know! There will be a clarity that is only true in Heaven. No more sluggish earthly mentality.

At present, I can still walk and breathe, but

one day my heart will stop. Maybe slowly—or instantly, as in Mavis's case. Nevertheless, it will stop one day, and I will be gone from this life forever. But I will be instantly *alive in Heaven*, free to enjoy every moment of it, free to experience everything before me. Only the Bible gives us a peek at what Heaven is like, an insight into understanding just a glimpse of eternity as described in that old spiritual, "What a day that will be/When my Jesus I shall see!"

Where we often find conflicting views in last-day doctrine, the Bible attempts to straighten us out. However, the Bible is in outline form, and it can be encumbered by interpretations and translations. The reality of Heaven will be infinitely better than any human brain can comprehend. It will be amazingly similar to what we read in scripture, because God's word is always accurate.

I am caught in a deep dilemma halfway between Heaven and earth. I am pulled downward and upward, not knowing which way is better.

I have always sought to blaze a trail in my life and ministry. Family and friends seem to understand and follow amazingly well, because it is simple and true. No matter the message, the best approach is to say it often, keep it simple, and make it burn. We have used that same approach, in a positive way, with simple tracts like the "Four Spiritual Laws" provided by Campus Crusade, later replaced by the equally simple "What Do You Think?" created by our ministry. It is easily understandable and has been pivotal in leading more than a million inmates to Christ.

In our ministry, I have been praying for God to raise up a whole new generation of committed leaders who will continue the work we began. In hopes of fulfilling that ideal, we have chosen Michael Nolan, a leader in Christian ministry for forty years, as our new CEO. His primary challenge will be to maintain the focus of the staff, which then motivates the local volunteer teams to carry out their responsibilities in each city. I am still exercising my leadership as founder and board member while trying to avoid stepping on the toes of other leaders in the ministry and continuing to lead in that most important area of development: fundraising. That task falls most heavily upon me. And even after my death, I am certain fundraisers will say to donors, "Bill will see you from Heaven and be pleased that you are continuing his legacy."

At age seventeen, I was faced with a dilemma: to call God and His Bible a lie or to turn in faith and call Him the Son of God and the only way to God and His eternal life. I chose Christ, and my life has proven to be wonderfully adventurous and miraculous by His leadership.

We can, at best, "only fake it until we make it," and we only make it when we have God on our team and in our life, deep inside of us! We are not just His followers. He is *living* inside of us. It's an inner leading. It's an inner job, done much like a man in a dark cave aided by a headlamp that only blinks when we are going the right way. At times, it's bright, and at times, it blinks on and off, green, yellow, and red. Green, go ahead. Yellow, slow down. Red, stop. Or full speed ahead—all kinds of commands. But I want to hear God's "full speed ahead" most of the time. I say wait for His leadership and it should always be clear, except when you *think* it isn't and a slowdown occurs: "For now we see through a glass, darkly" (1 Corinthians

> We are not just His followers. He is *living* inside of us.

13:12 KJV). But the fog will soon lift, and we'll then see more clearly and be able to go forward. We all must proceed slowly, not totally sure of the way to go on this earth. Lean strongly toward the Bible way! Watch for blinding lights. Stay on Heaven's clear path, where the lights are always bright and clear. Christ's light never dims in Heaven.

I once followed a hearse into a cemetery, and as it turned in, I noticed that the license plate read "U-2." *You, too,* must die and be buried six feet under. No one escapes death. We *all* die, possibly in a car wreck, a plane crash, a fiery explosion, or slowly, from a fatal disease. But sooner or later, "it is appointed for man to die once" (Hebrews 7:28 ESV). No one has *ever* escaped death. Someone once quipped, "Death and taxes are inescapable." You can't talk your way out of death—and that's for sure!

In my case, most of my body will be saved for spare parts, and what is left will be cremated and placed in a burial urn. But my spirit will be with the Lord in Heaven. Yes, death is truly inevitable, and so is Heaven or Hell, according to our Lord Jesus. Since death is coming for all of us, it's only a matter of when and how. Only God knows for sure when the doctor may say, "You've got two months or less to live in this world." You may linger for a while, but it will be soon. God said it in His word. It is a prophecy fulfilled for sure; human history agrees that there is no way out. Death's icy hand will put an end to your life. You may turn your back on God, but you can't back out on death! If you try to back out, you will back into your own grave.

But if you'll accept the Lord as your Savior you will walk out of the grave into eternal life! I pray you, like me, will have chosen the latter.

The end will just be the beginning. We will be eternal beings with God and Christ *forever*. How amazing that will be! Yes, yes, yes! God said it, I believe it, and that settles it. God and I will handshake and fist bump, and I'll get chill bumps.

In movies, the director will often shoot the ending first and build the story back to the beginning from there. The Lord reviews the ending in the Bible through Revelation: in the last days, wars and rumor of wars, men caring only for themselves, crazy weather, and horrific events. These are the end times, the tribulation and the conclusion of earthly history, the beginning of the Lord's thousand-year reign on this earth and in Heaven! This will take place so that the world will see He is Lord, reigning over all His creation forever and ever, amen!

CHAPTER 3
FISHING IN THE LAST DAYS

Since I believe we are in the last days, I am strongly convinced that we must pick the ripest fruit first. We can't wait for Sunday-school evangelism with its slowed-down pace, waiting for a certain age of accountability.

We must move quickly to gather souls, harvested at an increased speed. Jesus said He'd make us fishers of men, and we find the best fishing pond in prisons, where convicts are biting ravenously or even jumping in the boat! Lots of fish are anxious to take the bait.

We must learn to throw our nets on the other side of the boat like Peter, who, though he protested that they had fished all night and caught nothing, obeyed when Jesus told him to throw the nets on the other side of the boat. The resulting catch was so great that the boat began to sink from the large haul of fish (Luke 5:7).

In most prisons, the fires of Hell don't leap out on you, but there are doubled razor-wire fences twenty feet high, and the food is usually pretty bad. It is cooked and prepared by inmates. A lot of inmates choose to buy their food from the canteens, then heat it in their cells on hot plates, which seem to be available in most prisons. In the chow hall, the conditions are usually distasteful, but in most cases the food basically is pretty good even though preparations and service are poor. Prisoners can buy canteen food with their earnings from low-paying jobs or obtain it from visitors who sneak it in from the outside world. Obviously, this is not good, but anything is better than chow-hall food. Most inmates substitute canteen food for regular chow-hall food. So they're eating both but don't seem to be the worse for wear.

When I first met Jack Murphy, he was serving a twenty-one-year sentence. But since being converted, he has served on our staff for many years. He once bragged about making more money than the warden by selling drugs. His carefully pressed prison uniform and alligator shoes proved it.

When our ministry comes in, it is a breath of fresh air. We encourage teammates to eat with the prisoners in the chow hall. But our teammates avoid this because the food is not that tasty and probably because we do provide food for them at our Friday- and Saturday-night banquets. The food is generously donated by cooperating churches.

A PRAYER FOR BRUCE

It seems like people are dying around me all the time. Recently my son Bobby's father-in-law died.

Bruce Condor was in the last stages of diabetes.

Salvation is by faith, and so is healing, so I encouraged Bruce to pray. Here is the prayer I wrote for him:

Lord, relieve me of my great pain either in life or death. I know that in Heaven my foot and legs will be well, and I can run and dance on golden streets. In Heaven's fresh air, there will be no more tears or dying. Lord, I know my salvation is totally obtained by faith, and I believe this. I also know that healing is by faith, and I am seeking to believe this as well. Heal me from this miserable sickness and prepare me for Heaven, where my legs will be strong, and no more diabetes! The rot will be gone, replaced by your healing. Thank you, God. Amen!

I suggested that Bruce should pray this prayer over and over again, trusting God to replace his fear with faith. God can only answer a prayer of faith!

The pinnacle of my suffering was when Mavis died, but I revisited it at Bruce's death and that of other friends who are beating me to Heaven. There we will have relief from pain, and our earthly, cloudy thinking will be replaced by Heaven's complete healing. There, all earthly questions will be answered. In the meantime, I will have to be satisfied with only the partial scriptural understanding of so many questions and answers. But I am always thrown back in faith to believe that God's way is the best way for this life and the life to come. And

> There we will have relief from pain, and our earthly, cloudy thinking will be replaced by Heaven's complete healing.

I am obviously curious to know the beginning to the end—birth to death, which are the bookends to life. Our earthly life and eternal life are in between. Bruce's prayer was answered in his death on March 12, 2020.

CHAPTER 4
NUCLEAR DESTRUCTION

Now I will write of things in this life and life after death. In this life, I sometimes feel I have failed. I have met others with greater education and many with higher IQs. This sometimes causes me to feel inferior. But in the life to come, I will be inferior to no one. My body and brain will measure up to all others. If I have been given great goals to reach for by God in Heaven, then He will provide me with the tools to accomplish His goals. There will be no competition between me and God. We will always be on the same page. Obviously, He is infinitely above me in the accomplishment of His will. I will always be working with Him toward His great purposes. If there is a nail to drive, He'll provide just the right hammer. If there is a door to open, He will give me the key to the lock. The door

> If I have been given great goals to reach for by God in Heaven, then He will provide me with the tools to accomplish His goals.

will swing open wide, revealing the treasures within. Maybe I won't find silver or gold, but I will find whatever I need to help Him to accomplish His will on earth and in Heaven!

Healthcare providers were called upon daily during the recent coronavirus pandemic to give tests to check for coronavirus. It seemed that a lot of people thought they had contracted the deadly disease. But in most cases, they hadn't. Doctors and nurses were often awakened out of sleep for every sniffle and were asked, "Can I take the test?"

Doctors and nurses would try to put them off, pleading ignorance, but people still insisted on having the test. Even if the doctors could give the test and the person was cleared that same day, however, there was still the possibility of that person being sick.

But how would one know? The symptoms were deceptive; even the doctors said so. One might test negative but develop the disease the very next day. So the test would have to be done repeatedly in order to be sure that one was in the clear. The authorities said, "Save the test for the really sick!"

I decided not to take the test to give other people the chance to be tested. I have lived quite long enough. I am eighty-four! I will die from something other than the coronavirus.

But life is so fragile that we hang on to it by a thread. I weigh 218 pounds, and the string will break soon. I have lost some weight, but the thread is still frayed, and it will soon break. Life will end for me and every person on this floating ball in space. Sooner or later, life will end for all of us. No one escapes! Death can come suddenly, or, as in Bruce's case, slowly and with great pain. I pray for a quick death, but we don't always get to choose. Often loved ones grow tired of seeing us suffer and wish for a quick way out. But that prayer isn't always granted. The only thing I am sure of is death. I don't know when, or how, and neither does anyone else, even doctors. Only the Lord knows.

If there should be a nuclear exchange by small countries with a few nukes or large countries

Cape Canaveral anymore, because those both would be gone. All earthly cities would cease to exist. No earthly calls could be made because all life would be gone. You may protest that "no one could be that stupid." But Hitler, had he survived later in the Second World War, would have most likely detonated nuclear bombs on the free world. And there will always be that crazy Hitler type who would do so without fail. All of us would be speaking German if we had survived the nuclear exchange that would have followed. I don't even want to think about it! Did we escape by the skin of our teeth, or was it God's providence? Hitler brought us to the brink of nuclear war. Any rational person must be forced to this conclusion. But the odds have diminished. There are, at present, three big, powerful nations with unlimited nuclear power that could, at any time, pull the trigger on their nuclear warheads. Even worse, there are also many smaller nations that have seemingly unstable leaders who crave power and jealously want to take their place on the world stage.

Reducing the world to a radiation-filled swamp is their driving ambition. "If I can't have the world my way, then I'd rather not have it at all!" seems to be their thinking. What a way for our planet to end. And it *will* end. See the Book of Revelation with its fiery prediction of the last days! In 2 Timothy 3:1 we read, "But mark this: There will be terrible times in the last days" (NIV). We must pray that China and Russia will join our free world, and together we can prevent nuclear destruction. But the odds are greatly diminished because of nations that are determined not to be pushed around and often appear to be willing to destroy our planet to prove it.

CHAPTER 5
"FULL SPEED AHEAD!"

If I could show you a way that you could have a solution to all your problems, so that you could overcome death and have eternal life at the same time, you probably would jump at the chance. That's exactly what Christ has promised. All your sins can be forgiven by simply admitting that you are a sinner and trusting that Christ will do what He claims. This is done in an experience of rebirth. It can never be accomplished through our own human efforts and especially not through our good works. John 3:3 says, "Very truly I tell you, no one can see the Kingdom of God unless they are born again" (NIV). Philippians 3:9 also tells us to "be found in him, not having a righteousness of my own that comes from the law, but that which is through faith in Christ—the righteousness that comes from God on the basis of faith" (NIV). His salvation is now and forever, and there is no other way! He doesn't provide a choice of "either/or" but an *assurance* of forgiveness and eternal life. No man has ever made it right with God because of his own human effort. As sincere as he might be in living a good life, his sincerity is to no avail. It is only through a sincere trust in Jesus Christ and His death and resurrection that his salvation is assured. His sincerity only makes him sincerely wrong unless that sincerity leads to his pleading for forgiveness and eternal life through Christ alone. Only Christ promises forgiveness and eternal life. To believe is to be in life, and nothing else works.

The scripture says that "it is appointed for man to die once, and after that comes judgement" (Hebrews 9:27 ESV). Our appointed time is now. Some think that in order for something to be supernatural, it has to be weird. Faith is not a fact that we can pin down to our limited five senses. One day, God will provide answers to our questions. But we must have faith to believe beyond any earthly understanding!

But is that really knowing? Yes! How? By simply believing in what God says in His word. Having faith is the only way to God—not by sight but by faith. Having not yet seen, I believe by faith. No questions necessary—I just believe it! I know that the Lord cannot lie. He has told us, "Heaven and earth will pass away, but my words will never pass away" (Matthew 24:35 NIV).

Of course, I had to put Him to the test and remind myself that His truth is totally reliable, and He has kept His word! I have total trust in the Bible and in my experiences of answered prayer and His real leadership throughout my whole life.

I remember that when my first child, Billy, was born, the doctor agreed to let me watch through a big plate-glass window only a few feet away. When my son came out of his mother's womb, he opened only one eye and blinked with that eye at the light, which he was seeing for the first time. The light must have irritated him, having just come out of the darkness of the womb, because he blinked and that eye began to water. Then he opened both eyes. He seemed to adjust better to the blinding light, but began to cry and gasp for breath as the doctor grabbed him by his ankles and smacked him on the butt. I, too, breathed more freely, because I could see and hear that he was alive and well, and he has been for over half a century.

During his football career, my son Bobby complained to me: "I have size, speed, and everything it takes to be great in football, but I've been injured so much in my hip that I can't run without awful pain and can't block because of that or even worse pain in my shoulders. I know I've got what it takes to be a star in football, but my injuries make it impossible to do so. It's not fair!" Bobby and I got on our knees in frustration and prayed, "God, we hate to come to You complaining, but we have to admit that we don't feel that it has really been fair for Bob to have all of these injuries and not be able to play football at his best! If it isn't in Your will to heal his injuries, then show him what is in Your will." And God did exactly that, because my son was able to get married to a wonderful woman, was blessed with three great kids, and became very successful in business. What he didn't achieve in football he certainly made up for in his marriage, family, friends, and business. God did answer prayer, and it has been full speed ahead ever since! His "complaining" in the first part of his life was changed to thanksgiving in the second part.

What was my greatest victory in this life? Realizing my own sin, my lostness and faithlessness, and, most importantly, the power of Christ to save and forgive me for the great sins of selfishness and self-righteousness. I became too proud of never cheating in my marriage and being a good father and a wonderful grandfather and great-grandfather. Because of this, I wasn't attentive enough to the grandkids and great-grandkids. I was too anxious to give them money and things, and not anxious enough to give love and blessings in creative ways. Oh, I did give them enough in the way of saying it. "I love you" always came out so easily. But giving time and attention was more difficult. I still hope it's not too late! I'm certainly not too proud to take a chance on overdoing it. After all, I know that Mavis would be just as determined as I am, if not more so. I must make up for her being gone and be grandmother and grandfather on the Glass side. To be honest, the fact that Mavis and I expressed our love to each of the children was exceedingly helpful in making them better people. Even when we had to discipline them, the punishment was bookended before and after by saying, "I love you, but I love you too much to let your bad behavior go unpunished." The punishment was never too harsh, but it was harsh enough to get their attention. They all responded well, and I think this was because it was given in love. I would tell them, "My discipline hurts me more than it does you!" But I am certain they knew that my love never stopped or even wavered. When I was out of town, Mavis compiled a list of offenses for me to attend to upon my return.

to freely give us His total forgiveness! That's why He came to this planet two thousand years ago. The cross showed us His love and bought our forgiveness through His death. He paid the price for our sins. For us to try to pay the cost of what He did is impossible because He has already done it. Even if you thought you could repay, it would be foolish and counter-productive to try.

> For us to try to pay the cost of what He did is impossible because He has already done it.

When Mavis died, it was in the middle of the night from a sudden, thankfully painless, heart attack; for Bruce, it was painful and drawn out over many suffering days. For his loved ones, it was hard to see him suffer so drastically and for so long. They finally became weary of seeing him suffer so much. Before he left this "vale of tears," he could only bear the pain through heavy medication. And so we prayed, "Oh, God, please relieve his suffering. We can't take it any longer. Let him experience total healing in this life or in the life to come." You might protest, thinking this might seem like we were asking God to allow him to die. But we knew that he could take no more pain relievers other than the perfect one that comes with his exit from this life and entrance into life eternal. There, there will be no weeping and wailing and gnashing of teeth (Matthew 13:42)—just permanent relief from all pain. No morphine necessary! The tears and pain will be gone as he dances down the streets of gold.

You can't do anything toward salvation except to receive His free gift. You can try playing God, but it is foolish and will never work. It's like trying to paddle upstream at Niagara Falls. It's stupid! You are not a match for God and will only meet with complete destruction and hell.

Relax! Go to Heaven with a struggle only by surrendering to God! I gave up all human effort toward my salvation at age seventeen because I believed Christ's death and resurrection was enough to pay for my sins. And since following Him I have found the "yoke is easy and my burden is light" (Matthew 11:30 NIV). Things may not always be the way we want them to be, but His way is the best way. No more diabetes, no more swollen, blackened legs, no more stink of rotten flesh! Replaced only by freedom from pain and eternal life!

I am saved and have been chosen to follow Him to the ends of the earth and even beyond in Heaven. I bet it will be no picnic even in Heaven. There will still be battles to fight, but we'll have new powers to make us victorious. Even in those trials, we won't be without struggle! We will fight and win with a sense of a battle fought and won—not in a cloudy, floating environment but in a perfect world of victory and a victory of challenge achieved! And by our God-driven desires, we will fight on for His will and what He wants for His kingdom. Our earthly battles are behind us, and heavenly victories are a certainty. Worshipping God will be our most important goal.

I must move on and only hope that you can follow on from life and death to escape the bonds of this cursed, earthly drag and go on to the freedom that Heaven promises. To hold on enough to relate to earthly limitations, I can relate to the downward pull of earthly life. Yet the upward pull toward Heaven can draw us up to give a balanced solution to the spiritual upward pull. Hopefully, this will balance us so that we are never happy with a life that is too much in this world. Again, the answer is balance. We must be careful not to be so heavenly-minded that we are no earthly good.

When we are unbalanced, we cause others to be unbalanced between the two opposing pulls of earth and Heaven, becoming sickened even unto ourselves. We must move down our road of life, not leaning to the left or the right or up or down. It is easier to follow a balanced leader; otherwise there is confusion in the ranks. I know that my life on this earth is limited: I have already spent eighty-four years in this earth-bound atmosphere. But I hope this ministry can move along without my leadership. Other leaders could fill in very well, causing the ministry to move forward, even improving it. No ups or downs! No sharp rights or lefts! Just "full speed ahead"!

CHAPTER 6
FOOTBALL CARRYOVER

My beautiful wife, Mavis, unexpectedly died a short time after celebrating a great sixty-year marriage. Both of my parents felt the icy fingers of death as their lives were snuffed out too early. My dad died at forty-five from Hodgkin's disease, my mother at eighty-five from a fatal car wreck, my brother at seventy-five from cancer; and I miss them all desperately. I hate death and dying, but it is a part of life. Dying is the end of our lives on this earth but only the beginning of life eternal. Mavis's parents died in their eighties, and the rest of us will go the way of death also. We just don't know how or when. Thankfully, we will go on living and loving each other forever in eternity. The way we lived in this life will have certain impact on our lives after death. The way in which this life impacts eternity is debatable, but in what ways does it affect us in the life to come? Obviously, in our destiny and, less clearly, in the way we enjoy or dread life after death.

We can't expect to have an enjoyable life after death if our life has been lived without God! But if it has been lived for the Lord and with a concern for others, then it has been well spent, and we can look back on this life with joy and look forward to our reward in Heaven. In this life, believers shall suffer persecution. There is no way to escape it. In the life to come, we will be rewarded with victory! If we have spent this life serving the Lord, in Heaven there will be an awareness of whether we experienced victory in our life on earth. After we die, it is too late to make up for our shortcomings. We must be about the Master's business while still in this "vale of tears." It was Christ Himself who said, "Verily I say unto thee, today shalt thou be with me in paradise" (Luke 23:43 KJV). After we die, it will be too late. But Christ continues to remind us of "this day," so we must get started while we still have air in our lungs and the leadership of the Holy Spirit to light the way. Because Christ always gives us the "this day" warning, we know that time runs out quickly. There must be a setting of priorities, as Matthew 6:33 tells us: "But seek first His kingdom and His righteousness, and all these things will be given to you as well" (NIV). And the Bible does add all these things in their God-ordained order. Beyond

> We must be about the Master's business while still in this "vale of tears."

those two priorities, He doesn't tell us what numbers three through one thousand might be, but leaves it up to the Holy Spirit to give guidance. But obviously, we cannot live life by the numbers. We simply have to trust His leadership by faith. He will never leave us nor forsake us, and He has been faithful to me through the years. He keeps His word!

How does my football mental preparation carry over into the rest of my life?

I am very imaginative! That helped when I played football because I could play in my mind. I know that the Bible is correct: "A good man brings good things out of good stored up in his heart, and an evil man brings evil things out of the evil stored up in his heart. For the mouth speaks what the heart is full of" (Luke 6:45 NIV). In football, I always pictured myself playing great, and it came true (in all humility)!

lost weight; I am down to 218 pounds. When I played in the NFL, I weighed 270 pounds, but after my playing days, I dropped down to 250 pounds. But when this virus plagued us, I stayed at 218 pounds. I was just not hungry! I also coughed and ached and had shortness of breath. I even had a constant runny nose and didn't sleep much. My vivid imagination was working against me. I had faith in reverse. I had the curse, and the only way to stop it was to exercise my faith. I had to say to my body, "I have faith, and I am well and strong!" Satan was the cause of my "stinking thinking." I was well! This is the way out of these situations. All of us must refuse to believe the lies and speak truth and life to ourselves, and we will be victorious. Faith gives us the victory. Romans 10:17 tells us that "faith comes from hearing the message, and the message is heard through the word about Christ" (NIV). The only thing we can do is believe and receive "the righteousness that comes from God on the basis of faith" (Phil. 3:9 NIV). We had to pray in positive faith that this virus was no different than a case of the regular flu. We had to see it for what it is: a trick, a lie of the enemy to get us scared and off the track of keeping our faith in Christ.

We recently had a dilemma in our family. Just before the announcement that we were facing a worldwide pandemic, my fifteen-year-old niece, Georgi, was concerned about her salvation. She panicked because she feared disaster was coming during the pandemic, and she asked me to baptize her. She thought everyone was going to die. She knew that baptism was an outward showing of what you believe and that it alone would not get anyone to Heaven. We tried to convince her that everything was going to be OK and that everyone was not going to die. But she still insisted on being baptized. I called all of her family together and asked her to read a little tract that we use in the prisons titled "What Do You Think?" It explains in simple and yet powerful terms what the Bible says about being saved. The family joined her in reading the tract together and prayed with her and recorded the date of her accepting Christ as her Savior. I praised her decision to follow Christ in obedience to His command and be baptized. She didn't do it in order to be saved. Because she was now saved, she certainly wanted to be obedient and was simply doing what Christ commanded. She wasn't ashamed to proclaim to her family and the world that He was her Savior! So we took her to the pastor of our church and let him baptize her.

It was a beautiful Sunday afternoon during that coronavirus scare, and therefore only our immediate family was allowed to be present at the church. What a wonderful thing it was! She was immersed—totally submerged by our pastor, Bruce Zimmerman, who held her under until she bubbled!

There are those who believe that one must be immersed in the waters of baptism in order to be saved. In their thinking, baptism is a necessity for their rebirth and salvation. But salvation is only found in admitting one's own sins and repenting of them. Baptism is a totally separate thing because it is following in obedience to the Lord's command to be baptized. As Georgi understood, baptism is not a requirement for one's salvation. Rather, it is a growth step of obedience, just as you should pray, read your Bible, be faithful to your church, and follow Christ in all other areas of Christian growth. Salvation is possible without baptism, as evidenced by the thief on the cross who died next to Jesus. He had no opportunity to be baptized or experience any Christian growth. Yet he was saved as Christ promised him: "Truly I tell you, today you will be with me in paradise!" (Luke 23:43 NIV). You should be baptized, but it has no

CHAPTER 7
"GLORY HALLELUJAH"

The last two books I have written were different from the others. Due to a stroke knocking out my ability to read and edit, I hired an assistant in his mid-fifties to help me. Tony grew up on the East Coast in Maryland and Delaware. His grandparents lived through the Great Depression and would tell him stories of how tough things were back then. They supplemented their income by traveling and singing in churches everywhere on the East Coast. It wasn't a lot of money, but it helped support them during that time. One afternoon in March, Tony and

I engaged in a long conversation about an old spiritual, and I asked him if he remembered a song that went something like, "What a day that will be/When my sweet Jesus I shall see!" He explained how his grandmother would sing a lot of old hymns as he grew up and that song was one of them. "When We All Get to Heaven" is what he said it was called, and he began to sing it for me, not missing a word or note of the song, recalling all of it. When he was done our eyes were tear-filled. Tony is more than an assistant; he is a friend whom I call my buddy, and sometimes he pokes fun at me. I love to tease him by saying he's my brother from another mother. During the song he made fun of my horrible voice, so I would hum along with him while he would sing loudly.

It was as if he were drowning out the noise that his granddad's Ford Model A would make as he drove down the road, just like his grandmother, when she practiced before her engagements, sang loudly to drown out that same noise.

We can know that as surely as we die, we will wake up in Heaven as the song says. We will see our sweet Jesus and all those who died in Christ before us. I'm looking forward to a great reunion with teammates from football days and ministry teammates as well. We will reminisce about all of those victorious days and disastrous days also. But since we will be in Heaven, there's always that great ending to the story: we will have won! And the Bible says that we will be given crowns as our reward, not crowns of thorns, but crowns of righteousness (2 Timothy 4:8). We will cast our crowns at God's feet. Our rewards are only deserved by Him!

Revelation shows us what worship in Heaven looks like: "The twenty-four elders fall down before Him who sits on the throne and worship him who lives forever and ever. They lay their crowns before the throne and say: 'You are worthy, our Lord and God, to receive glory and honor and power, for you created all things, and by your will, they were created and have their being'" (4:10 NIV). Creatures around the throne also give praise, saying, "Holy, holy, holy, is the Lord God Almighty, who was, and is, and is to come" (Revelation 4:8 NIV). He was in the beginning; He is in the present, and He is to come in the future! *Maranatha.*

The Bible comes to a climax with the end of the world. Then comes the new world, which is Heaven. In this life, our world will come to an end with a seven-year tribulation followed by a thousand-year reign by our Lord. Satan will be thrown into a fiery pit! After the thousand years, all Christians will be caught up to live with Him in Heaven forever.

There are those like Randy Alcorn, in his book titled *Heaven*, who think that there will still be battles to fight and victories to be won after the end of the world. There are questions that I would want to ask. If Satan is cast into Hell, who will the opposition be? It will be a simple matter of winning the battle. We will in time understand fully: "For now we see through a glass, darkly; but then face to face: now I know in part; but then shall I know even as also I am known" (1 Corinthians 13:12 KJV). Thankfully, I will see clearly and understand completely what God had in His mind from the beginning. Apart from this earthly limited thinking, the fog will be lifted. I will win a great victory over my own ignorance! But God will not hold me accountable for ignorance. He'll give me grace. Salvation is never based on merited favor, but it is always based on unmerited favor. It is a gift. By definition, we can't merit a true gift already bought and paid for. By His death and resurrection, it has been paid in full!

Christians down through the ages have made the Roman centurion famous for his statement: "Surely this man was the Son of God!" (Mark 15:39 NIV). Mark also points out that the soldiers under his command confirmed this. Christians have affirmed down through the centuries that the only way to get to God is through Jesus.

In the last moments of Jesus's death, the sky grew densely black, and the Roman soldiers' torches flickered in the darkness. The terrible, thick blackness was only pierced by His last words on the cross: "It is finished" (John 19:30 NIV). This great act by Christ was followed three days later by His resurrection from the grave. Hallelujah, Christ arose! I want to preach to everyone everywhere and spread the gospel to the ends of the earth, and so should all the people of God do likewise. "Even so, come, Lord Jesus!" (Revelation 22:20b NKJV). Let us use this time before come to Him by faith. But I can't use His sovereignty as an excuse to not share the good news with others. Christ died and rose again that all might find forgiveness in Him! That's why Christ came to our world over two thousand years ago. Not just to say, "I love you and want you to come be with me to live forever in a perfect place called Heaven," but also to say, "I'm going to purposely lower myself long enough to die and be raised from the dead in order to save you." I must ask, "Jesus, was it so important to put yourself through the suffering of death and resurrection?" I think if I were God, I could have come up with a better way! But He didn't. Quit fighting God's will, I tell myself. He is God; He is right. He chose to suffer a painful death and resurrection. I do know the best way is His way. He can see what I can't see. He has done what I couldn't do for myself, and He knows what I don't know until I see Him face-to-face! What He has done can't be improved upon, but I must admit, He surely didn't choose the easy way!

He is preaching a profound truth to us. The message is simple: if you want to save the world, you must pay a steep price. You have to come down from Heaven and put yourself through Hell. "To set the masses free," you must get your hands and feet bloody by being nailed to an "old rugged cross" and be willing to suffer as He has suffered for us!

> The message is simple: if you want to save the world, you must pay a steep price.

I still think I could have come up with a better way to save us, a less painful way, but I am just a mere man. I am not God! I realize my resistance to doing it His way is not godly. It's just that I wanted Him to suffer less! Suddenly I realize that is what Peter wanted—and Jesus called him "Satan"!

If He had suffered less, if He didn't go to the cross, would that have made our salvation void? No, I am hiding behind my own way of thinking, trying to protect Jesus Christ from His own death. Stupid! Yes, stupid—I should know better! How foolish. His way is always right, always the best way. Our way of thinking, unless led by the Holy Spirit, will get us into trouble.

The universe demands a maker, and a great creation demands a great creator, which will always bring us back to God. Glory and amen!

CHAPTER 8
WEDGE BUSTER

We keep coming back to the downward pull that is so characteristic of this world—this worldly drag of worries, of sin, and of death, interspersed with minor victories and major defeats. Do not let it pull you down. We selfishly want to be transported into that wonderful place called Heaven and dodge all the struggles of this world. God allows us to suffer here, all the while shaping us into His image, hardening us for life's battles. It is no pillow fight. It is a slugfest, with bloody noses and broken teeth, but we will emerge victorious.

I am still encumbered with the need to relate to this lost world that so desperately needs a Savior. There is one great plus: there is still enough time to snatch a few lost sinners before the clock runs out! Let's win as many as possible for the Lord, before it is too late. Scripture teaches that there will be a great falling-away, motivating believers to bring about a new evangelistic awakening. At least that revival is what I am praying for, and I certainly want to be prepared to be one of those evangelists who will be used by God to help in that great gathering during the last days.

The way back is always the way it was in the first place, by grace through faith. This is not of ourselves but in surrendering to the will of Christ. It is never by our human effort but by His finished work. There is always that ongoing propensity to attempt to merit His grace, but this is a big lie of the enemy that must be arrested quickly. The only thing that makes Satan a little easier to defeat is his pre-dictability. He seems to use the same tactics repeatedly. If we pay attention to his pattern, we should be able to overcome the lies and see the truth. Having faith in God and the grace He has given us is Satan's downfall and our key to victory. I am a churchgoer, a Bible reader, and a lover of God's commandments. No wonder the enemy has tried to stop me in my tracks so many times. But faith has kept me moving forward and farther

> Having faith in God and the grace He has given us is Satan's downfall and our key to victory.

into God's wisdom. God promises life, where Satan's goals are destructive: "The thief [Satan] has come to steal and kill and destroy; I [Jesus] have come that they may have life and have it to the full" (John 10:10 NIV).

The enemy can't have anything unless

we let him. Remember we belong to Christ. Nothing can touch us unless God allows it!

As we found Him in our rebirth, we must grow in Him continuously by grace through faith. I keep being confronted with that trap because I really want to sidestep. I don't want to face that brute power coming at me like a locomotive with teeth flashing and destruction assured. So I must ask Him: what must I do to be spared from that impending defeat?

It is true of all of us—not just me as an evangelist, but you as a businessman, or as a housewife, and all committed Christians. We must all ask a question: "How do I fit into your last-day plans, Lord?" No one should be left out! I got a call from one of our teammates, and he said, "I am convinced that we are living in the last days, and I want to be sure not to be left out of God's plan for the great awakening that the Lord predicts in Revelation and many other last-day prophecies." We should all prepare in the same way.

power forward, following the center. Second, he could hand off the ball to the right running back, or, third, to the left running back. All three plays would power up the middle. The Wedge was always good for short yardage but was also successful for kickoffs, field goals, and extra points. We stomped our way to victory, shoulder to shoulder, with locked arms, elbow to elbow. Coach Bill Stages was famous for the Wedge. It had been used before in college football, but never in high school. He was the first to use it, and we thought he was a genius.

For extra points, a running back would use the apex of the wedge to spring off the center's shoulder pads to wildly block the extra point at least ten feet in the air. We called this the "Flying Wedge." When the opponents had the ball, we would call it the "Superman Wedge," and in much the same way, the defensive back would spring off the shoulders of the lineman at the point of the wedge and bound into the opposition backfield. He had no cape, but he flew amazingly high and usually landed astride the opposing running back, wildly knocking him to the ground! This often caused fumbles or stopped them cold in their tracks, usually knocking the running back unconscious. But in any event, it was a mighty collision. Our coach kept inventing new ways to use the Wedge, like on the kickoff, which was called the "Super Wedge." We all flew down the field forming a big V—the coach dramatized it by calling it our "V for victory." It really was like the original Wedge except that we had a running start, giving us even more momentum with our shoulder-to-shoulder and elbow-to-elbow interlocking brute force! It allowed the kick returner to go much faster and leap even higher.

The Wedge was great for kickoffs, and when our adversaries were caught off guard, it truly was a power play. With that extra running force, we locked arms and flew down the field, knocking the opposition to the right or left or slinging them backward. It worked great early in the season, until our opponents figured out a way to slow down the Wedge.

Football history is filled with trick plays like the Wedge, which was magical and, for a while, unsolvable. There was a trick pass play called the Statue of Liberty, and for a while, it faked everyone out. This was when the quarterback would toss the ball to the running back, and the running back would fake a pass by holding up the ball high above his head. The other running back would come up behind him and grab the ball, then run around him to the goal line. And there you have the Statue of Liberty!

Yeah, unfortunately, our opposition finally came up with what they called the "Wedge Buster."

There is always the "Wedge Buster" with Satan. Just when you think that you have the right play, Satan can always devise an atomic bomb or some other "germ warfare" type of play to offset your Wedge! Football usually comes down to blocking and tackling. The great pass play demands a Statue of Liberty to fake you out or the Wedge Buster to slow you down. You can't seem to ever overcome the unstoppable, perfect play. There is always a way to defeat your trick plays, so football keeps coming back to the fundamentals of blocking and tackling. It is seldom that you can win by trickery. Trick plays can always be broken up. You can't trick your way to victory! The enemy will always figure out a way to destroy you unless you put on the whole armor of God that Ephesians 6:13 describes. Satan is a formidable foe.

> The enemy will always figure out a way to destroy you unless you put on the whole armor of God.

To my amazement I lately came across the word "persnickety," the favorite word of my coach, Bill Stages. It means "unnecessarily difficult."

He would say, "I don't mean to be persnickety," and I never really knew what it meant until recently. I thought it was just a slang word that he used, but it was a good word that I recently found, of all places, in the dictionary.

My old coach was right as usual. He would bring us in thirty minutes early, not to talk about football but to lecture us about the importance of positive thinking and having good values and manners. I learned a lot about football from him and even more about public speaking, which I have used to great advantage for over sixty years. Coach Stages had an excellent vocabulary and punctuated his speeches with a lot of humor, which kept the attention of our group of easily bored teenagers. His inspiring words have stuck with me for more than half a century.

Boris Johnson, the prime minister of Great Britain, bragged about being so unafraid of the coronavirus that he ignored his own directives and that of the United States as well. He continued to touch his constituents by shaking hands with them. For once our president was more careful; he refused to shake hands with anyone and washed his hands constantly after being around others, including his own staff.

He was extremely wise to adhere to his own guidelines. Thank God that Boris didn't have to pay for his actions by giving up his life. He contracted the virus, but he did survive.

For a change, our president isn't playing the daredevil, but has taken a more conservative stance and is obeying the "six-foot rule." It would be foolish to do otherwise!

I am so glad that two great world leaders, the prime minister and our president, are coming to this wise conclusion of adhering to the "six-foot rule" and using this last-day prophecy to herd as many people as possible into Heaven and fantastic victory. As I said before, "When we all get to Heaven, what a day of rejoicing that will be!"

I am certain that the prime minister and the president are not great evangelists, but I do believe that they will figure into this last-day gathering, either because of themselves or in spite of themselves. I am certain that God can even use a donkey! Surely if God can use a donkey—and even more accurately a jackass— to speak to Balaam, surely He can use the prime minister and the president to speak to the pagan people of this world in the last days.

God is in the business of using unlikely people to accomplish fantastic miracles. He used a carpenter to be reincarnated as the Son of God, and He used a jackass to speak to Balaam (Numbers 22:28).

Paul was the greatest evangelist that ever lived, and he was certainly an unlikely person to be so. At the beginning, he went about killing Christians. But the blinding light on the road to Damascus changed him completely. He ended up writing much of the New Testament and became the greatest evangelist of all time. If God can save even Paul and make him into a great evangelist, surely He can use you and me!

Personally, I am certain that I am more like Balaam's jackass because of my ineptitude. I lack the polish of Billy Graham or the ability of Paul. But if He can use even a jackass, he can use me. None of us can hide behind a lack of ability. Even Moses stuttered and was a poor speaker, but God provided Aaron, his brother, to be his spokesman (Exodus 4:10, 14).

Fred Smith was my favorite person in this world. He was like a father to me! He was a second father after my dad, who died at the young age of forty-five. I was fourteen when he died.

I met Fred when I was a twenty-two-year-old senior at Baylor. I learned more from my second father, Fred, than from my actual dad. But my real dad was gone. He died when I was still an immature teenager. He suffered from Hodgkin's disease. He grew weaker and lost so much weight that he went down from 205 pounds to 125 pounds. But he was always loving and positive with me and all of his family and friends.

I had to be brave for my mom and two-year-old sister, Linda. My dad instructed me many times while on his deathbed. He would say, "Don't let Linda run into the street and get hit by a car! Take care of your mother and Linda. You'll be a great football player like your brother." He would drill those things into my head constantly and with a lot of love.

In the last stages of Hodgkin's disease, your joints hurt and you are in a lot of pain. The only way to relieve my dad's pain was to bring hot towels and place them on his joints, shoulders, knees, and every moving part that hurt the most. The hot towels helped to alleviate the pain—the hotter, the better.

My dad would brag on me a lot, saying that I brought the hottest towels that really helped the most. I was so determined to get the towels hot, hotter than anyone else, but the downside was that I burned my hands wringing out the hot water. But if it helped my dad, I didn't care—anything for him!

I haven't mentioned how Fred and my dad were different. Fred broadened my mind about the difference between the racially segregated South and the true Christian position, which is to love men regardless of their skin color. It is important to include all people in evangelism and every other phase of Christian endeavor and to oppose all forms of prejudice. This is the true meaning of "becoming all things to all men" (1 Corinthians 9:22). He insisted that I shouldn't confuse southern prejudice and genuine Christianity. This was especially important because I had become a spiritual leader on my campus and other universities. He affirmed that I must take the Christian position and not the racially prejudiced position of the South. Where there is conflict, the Christian position must be favored over prejudices of any kind.

I had become a famous football player as an All-American and first draft choice going to the pros, and I was a Christian leader, like it or not. Fred pointed out that I didn't have the luxury of opposing the true Christian position as opposed to the prevailing prejudice. He was constantly reminding me of the sin of prejudice of any kind.

I spent most of my time between the ages of twelve and fourteen keeping Linda out of the streets and wringing out hot towels.

I was always running back and forth between Dad's room and the bathroom in that middle-class neighborhood of Corpus Christi, Texas. I kept the towels so hot that I had to be careful not to burn his skin, which by then was numbed by the pain and easily burned because of his thinness. He had always had an athletic body, but for the last two years, he was a skeleton of what he had been—a pro baseball pitcher in the Texas League, only one step below the big leagues. This was Triple-A baseball. Many friends of my dad's bragged about how great he was as a leftie pitcher who really was good enough for the big leagues. He had retired early because of his growing family. He had a devotion to his wife and kids, and he worked hard at growing a number of businesses in a thriving little town.

I remember standing by a big potbelly stove, listening to the old men tell stories. Some were true and others a big lie. If my dad rolled his eyes in the back of his head, that story was a lie. If he shrugged his shoulders, that meant he wasn't sure if it was true or not. Over time I learned to tell good stories, but my seminary professors insisted that we always tell the truth. Those old men around that stove could tell the most fantastic tales. They weren't limited by having to be true. At the end of each tall tale, they would spit on the red-hot stove, and it would sizzle and smoke.

In the NFL, there were some big bull shooters just about as good at telling stories as those old men and even better at spitting. They did less lying, but not by much. Teammates would call them out if the story was too hard to believe. If your teammate got out of balance with a lie, there was always someone to call him out and make him tell the truth. If an argument broke out, it would be settled with a wrestling match or a fistfight.

But the coach would yell, "Come on! Save it for Sunday against the Bears!"—or whoever we were playing—which always brought us back to the reality of the opponents we were facing in the following game. After all, we were on the same team.

That coach pointed out the obvious. You have to figure out who your opponents are and who your teammates are. It's easy in football, yet it is so difficult in life. Satan is often disguised; he appears to be beautiful at times, as with Delilah tempting Samson. Drugs look so good—alcohol gives you a buzz. But in the end, it stings like an adder.

Satan often looks so good at first. Many country western singers like Glen Campbell and Johnny Cash died from drug or alcohol addiction. Many athletic stars are doing the same thing.

They fall for the lie. They see the satanic lifestyle as attractive but, in the end, it has a deadly bite!

I played with one of the greatest quarterbacks that ever played the game. His name was Bobby Layne. In one of my early years in football, I was the offensive center, which demanded that he put his hands between my legs. We were at close range, so I could always smell the stench of alcohol on his breath and body. It didn't seem to affect his athletic ability that much—except that he died at an early age.

It's important not to confuse teammates with an opponent. They have a different-colored jersey. They are the enemy. Satan is our enemy and Christ our teammate. Never should the two be confused. Know what team you are on. Even in practice, when we were all on the same team, we would pose as opposing teams by wearing different-colored jerseys. We were taught to hate our opponents and love our teammates. After games we would shake hands and be cordial, but we would maintain our competitive feelings toward our opponents. We seldom fought in practice because the coach would yell, "Save it for the Bears on Sunday!" This cut down the fighting during practice.

Educational level had little to do with how often fights broke out in games or in practice. Our quarterback, Dr. Frank Ryan, had an earned doctorate from Rice. He later taught at Rice and Yale. Every player had a college degree, and many had at least a master's degree, and I was a seminary graduate. But we all got in fights at one time or another. Football is a violent game, and it would be a shame to take all the fight out of players. Even though at their best they may be ashamed of their tendency toward violence, it is a built-in danger in any violent game. The animal in us tends to stick his ugly head out at times. But the angel in us ends up shaking hands.

God did not create us and leave us alone, but gave us the best clues in the Bible to show us how to live.

> **God did not create us and leave us alone, but gave us the best clues in the Bible to show us how to live.**

It is a matter of record that I played twelve years, one year in Canada and then in the NFL in the sixties and seventies for eleven years. I was selected to the Pro Bowl four times, made the All-American team in college, and was drafted number one by the Detroit Lions. That record allowed me to have a great football career.

God expected me to use that fame in the best possible way to reach the most people for Christ.

Even after being retired for over fifty years, I still receive fan mail daily, and I am faithful in returning my autograph to fans.

God has allowed me to be in many halls of fame, but the only one I care about is having my name written in the Lamb's Book of Life!

I know I'm not a great author. Then you ask, "Why write? This just proves your lack of ability."

I have written thirteen books in order to leave a lasting imprint. All the recognitions that I can ever accumulate will never amount to anything except that the Lord can use it to touch others.

I was watching an interview done by the fourth draft choice of the Dallas Cowboys. Reggie Robinson was so excited to tell the story of receiving a personal phone call from Jerry Jones, the Dallas Cowboys owner. I noticed that a lot of great athletes appear to be unconcerned about their influence. But Pilate, that pagan ruler over Judaea during the life of Christ, could not escape his influence and accountability. Neither can I or anyone else escape our influence. Like Pontius Pilate we have to say, "What I have written, I have written" (John 19:22 NIV).

The only hall of fame I want to make is God's. But the most famous or the humblest of us must still give an account. There is no way to rationalize it or avoid responsibility. There are many athletes, both in my era and today, who want to escape accountability. They will have to conclude at the end of life: "It is impossible."

The Sadducees and Pharisees wanted to argue with the title that Pontius Pilate nailed to the cross, which was, "JESUS OF NAZARETH, THE KING OF THE JEWS" (John 19:19 NASB). They wanted to change it to say that He only claimed to be the King of the Jews, but Pilate doggedly stuck to his word.

Every person must agree with Pilate that their lifetime demands honesty because it is written on every page. In the movie *The Ten Commandments*, after his defeat at the Red Sea,

Pharaoh has to admit, "His God is God!"

When Jesus was asked how to judge the woman caught in adultery, He said, "Let any one of you who is without sin be the first to throw a stone at her" (John 8:7 NIV). Not one person threw a stone. We all must drop our stones because we all have sinned. We have broken all ten commandments either by action or by thought.

No matter how many times we try, we cannot escape accountability. It is like trying to beat the train, but you hit the fiftieth car or even the caboose. We are not even close!

Our only hope is to desperately plead for His forgiveness, because we all are guilty by action or thought. When Christ expanded His commandment to include thought, we all hit the caboose. It is not a narrow miss. We are complete disasters. We must sing that old song, "Not by our own self-righteousness but to the cross we cling."

As the soldiers stood around the cross, I would say it was a universal decision that everyone agreed He was the Son of God. It was impossible to watch the Son of God on the cross and not believe! Jesus was dying for all of us sinners (John 3:16–17).

It was so real. God was intervening on our behalf. He was interfering with human history, causing it to shake the very foundation of creation, spiritually and physically causing the dead to rise during the crucifixion (Matthew 27: 51–52).

Jesus paid for the very sins of which we are all guilty, past, present, and future. He covered them all with His blood, His very life, giving us a bridge to have an everlasting relationship with the Father. He has performed a finished work!

This seems to be the last days, but scripture leaves a lot of room to argue. Are we really in the "last days"? Is the "last days" a year or a thousand years? I don't know, and neither do you.

When is the Lord coming back? I am betting soon, but who knows? No matter when He returns, "we know that all things work together for good to them that love God, to them who are called according to his purpose" (Romans 8:28 KJV).

Suppose He is delaying His coming so millions can make their way into the Kingdom of God. Maybe delaying long enough for our grandchildren to make it across the finish line before it is too late!

Who can say when the world will end, except God? Our death will stop our opportunity to get right with God.

I went walking after the virus death toll had soared into the thousands. Only in 1918 had it been worse. We thought that in this modern age of advanced medicine there was no way it could be that bad, but it was. It was a hurricane. Worse yet, there is no vaccine for COVID-19. There is no miracle like the polio shot to stop it in its tracks! Hopefully soon there will be a cure discovered. We keep searching for the vaccine. God knows that every doctor and scientist in the world will be in search of the miracle vaccine that can be placed in a shot to cure it once and for all.

Hopefully, men will not be so foolish as to let another deadly virus be turned loose on the world. However, when we developed the atomic bomb, we thought no one would release it into the world, but we were wrong.

What if there were hundreds of viruses set loose in the world? It would be worse than thousands of nuclear bombs being set off at once. I pray that no man or nation would be that foolish, but who knows? Men are desperately wicked. Our only hope is a wholesale turning to God, which would cause men to love and not hate others. In fact, I would go a step farther and pray for a spiritual awakening!

I went walking after being cooped up for days inside for fear of the virus. When I heard people talking about God, I thought, *What a great thing. They must have been talking about God because the virus brought them to the realization of needing God!* But then I listened more carefully. They were talking about God, but they were only using His name in vain.

The spring air was crisp, and their language was so shocking, even though the worst of the cussing was among the men. The women were loudly laughing their approval. This was not just in my neighborhood. I am sure in most neighborhoods it is the same.

We want to get out and stretch our wings

and cuss up a storm! No true Christians are like this. But Satan is alive and well.

I pray that the Roosevelts and the Churchills will always win out against the Hitlers. Most historians agree that Hitler was the only German leader who really wanted war. But he was so wicked that he overpowered those who opposed it. He was virtually the only leader in Germany, and so he prevailed, forcing the entire nation to follow him in his craziness. Only God can intervene and cause the Roosevelts and Churchills to win out in the end. I must believe that God's will shall be ultimately done. Before I close my book, I simply have to say that I wouldn't want to be "persnickety," because I am certain that God will prevail.

Years ago, I was invited to go down to Australia to conduct some citywide crusades in Melbourne, Sidney, and Wagga Wagga, spending seven days in each. I like the Aussies. They were a lot like Texans. There was a doctor there (an MD) about my age who became a good friend. We decided to go for a jog. I needed the workout to stay in shape. He led me on a jog through the woods on a rough trail. It was amazing and beautiful as he took me through mud and over rocks, up and down hills and valleys on uncharted trails, onward through the roughest terrain. Later, I asked him why he chose such a rough trail. He explained that he had been trying to make it as hard as possible to test me and see if I was as great an athlete as my publicity had made me out to be. Surely, I could make it in Australia, being an All-American pro football player. A rough terrain should be no problem for me.

He seemed to be a nice gentleman, well-educated with his MD degree. He used the King's English extremely well. But he was a tough competitor and enjoyed the challenge of seeing if I could pass the endurance test.

To top it off, the next day this tough little Aussie doctor worked me out with a boomerang. I was still sore from the rough jog the day before. He was great with the boomerang, and I was a novice. He threw it out hard and fast, and it would sail gently back to him. He would snag it with one hand. It was so easy for him. But when I tried, I could never get it to come back! I had to chase down my errant throws, and he would giggle at my lack of ability. I had to give up in disgust. I could play football, but I was poor with the boomerang! That Aussie doctor told me I could preach, but I wasn't any good in Aussie sports! I would never be an Aussie sports pro, to say the least.

There is a boomerang effect on our lives, I'm sure assigned by God. But even the pagan governor of Judaea, Pontius Pilate, found it hard to escape the truth. What you have written in your life keeps coming back at you. Pilate may very well have turned out to be a believer.

No one could talk him out of believing that the man he gave the order to be crucified was not the "KING OF THE JEWS" (John 19:19).

He agreed with the centurion and other soldiers who watched Jesus dying on the cross along with other Christians that Jesus was the Son of God. I truly believe it, not only because of the overwhelming evidence in history and the Bible, but because of my own personal experience as a genuine Christian.

ABOUT THE AUTHOR

Bill Glass was one of the most outstanding football players in the NFL. He was a unanimous All-American at Baylor University and a member of the College Football Hall of Fame. After one year in Canadian football, he enjoyed an eleven-year NFL career with the Detroit Lions and Cleveland Browns and was a four-time Pro Bowl selection. During his time with the Browns, Bill spent his off-seasons studying for a degree in theology at Southwestern Seminary.

After hanging up his jersey, Glass founded the Bill Glass Ministries in 1969, at the urging of his close friend Billy Graham. Today, through his program Bill Glass Behind the Walls, Bill has shared the Word of God with thousands of inmates and is the founder and leader of one of the world's oldest and largest prison ministries.

Bill has three grown children—Billy, Bobby, and Mindy—and eight grandchildren. They live near Dallas, Texas.

Bill and Mavis Glass (just married)

Mavis and Bill speaking with a gentleman

Bill, Bobby, Billy, Mindy, and Mavis (family portrait)

EVANGELIST — Bill Glass, former All-American college
Pro football star, was the evangelist for the Greater Ind
Crusade for Christ held Oct. 25-Nov. 1 at the State Fair C
Nearly 60,000 attended the eight services.

Indianapolis

Newspaper Report

dianapolis Crusade

970 —60,000 attend

T. 25 Nov. 1st —820 decisions

than 12,000 Indianapolis area
ts filled the State Fair Coliseum for
sing service Nov. 1 of the Greater
apolis Crusade for Christ, bringing
tendance for the eight-night campaign
rly 60,000, according to crusade of-

y reports indicate that 820 public
ns were registered by those respond-
the invitation at the close of each
service.

cher for the crusade was Bill Glass,
professional football player. Glass is
fulltime evangelist, after retiring from
ll last year.

s is a native of Corpus Christi, Tex.,
w makes his home in Waco, Tex. He is
luate of Baylor University in Waco,
he was an All-American football
, and Southwestern Baptist Theological
ary, Fort Worth, Tex.

r playing several seasons in Canada,
played with the Detroit Lions and the
and Browns. With the Browns he was
i to several All-Pro teams as defensive

Indianapolis crusade was Glass' third
diana in about 18 months. Similar
aigns were held in Evansville April 1969
Terre Haute October 1969.

sic for the Indianapolis crusade was led
b Harrison of San Francisco, Calif. The
ne soloist also directed the 2,000-voice
which sang nightly.

ss also shared the platform with dif-
individuals who gave testimonies each
These were:

Lt. Clebe McClary, highly-decorated
Marine veteran.

Dale Evans, actress wife of Roy Rogers.

Ray Hildebrand, recording star who's
record "Hey Paula" sold over three-million
records.

John Westbrook, former football star.

Craig Baynham, halfback for the Chicago
Bears.

Suzanne Johnson, former Miss Illinois.

Tom Lester, who is "Eb" on the television
series, "Green Acres."

In addition to the nightly services Glass and
team members spoke at Indianapolis-area
high schools and civic clubs.

Clyde Dupin, former pastor of Trinity
Wesleyan Church, Evansville, was director of
the crusade. He reports that more than 130
churches were actively involved with the
crusade to the degree that they provide
people for committees. He estimates that
about 200 churches were involved in some
aspect of the crusade.

Counselor training sessions were held for
seven weeks prior to the crusade with 1,500
counselors attending the required number of
sessions. These counselors and churches are
now participating in an extensive follow-up to
conserve the results of the crusade.

The budget for the Greater Indianapolis
Crusade was $75,000. The crusade office
reports that the budget has nearly been
reached and there are other pledges still
coming in.

Indianapolis Mayor Richard Lugar
welcomed the crusade and presented a "key
to the city" to Bill Glass at the opening night
service.

Mavis and Bill with grandkids

Michael Nolan, CEO of Bill Glass Behind the Walls

Larry Foster, former board member & great friend

Wayne R. Stevenson, former board member & great friend

Lou Korom, former board member & great friend

Bobby (son) and Bill Glass

Billy and Laura Glass,

Chairman of the Board, Bill Glass, Behind the Walls

Bill and Mindy Glass (daughter)

Miki Canada (editor)

Amy Canada (artist, front cover)